Wick Harbour
and the Herring Fishing

Wick Harbour
and the
Herring Fishing

by

Iain Sutherland

Illustrated with

Johnston Photographs

Photographic Selection by

William Lyall

Acknowledgements

The Wick Society is indebted to Mr James P. Campbell of Halkirk for his technical advice and assistance with the reproduction of prints from the original negatives.

Photographs

Published by Camps Bookshop, Wick and The Wick Society.
Printed by The Northern Times, Golspie.
© Text: Copyright Iain Sutherland.

Introduction

There was a day when the name of the town of Wick, or more accurately Pulteneytown, symbolised the very soul of the herring fishing industry. It was to herring what Dundee was to jute, Glasgow to shipbuilding and Edinburgh to architecture.

Many writers, both the local press correspondents and visiting observers, tried to convey in words the breathtaking scenes which unfolded before them with the arrival or departure of the fishing fleet which streamed in long lines to the horizon and beyond. A spectacle which was beyond the skills even of Robert Louis Stevenson, who could only watch, awestruck by the sheer indescribable scale of events.

There were others who did try, groping around for a suitable word. " Herringopolis," one suggested. Another " The Herring Capital of Europe." Pulteneytown was indeed both these things but neither description conveyed the atmosphere. Yet others attempted to sketch the scene for the imaginations of their readers but soon found themselves running out of superlatives and had to give up with an exhausted talent which had collapsed after a page or so.

But one man, the first of three, two of whom were to follow him over the next hundred years or so into the family business, succeeded in recording the scene in a way with which the writers could not compete. He also wrote. But he wrote with light and shadow and his instrument was a strange box with a brass tube sticking out of one side, which he pointed at the scenes before him.

This book contains samples of what he, his son and grandson, described.

Iain Sutherland,
Chairman,
The Wick Society.

Alexander Johnston (Frontispiece) founder of the firm of A. Johnston & Son, Photographers.

The Johnstons — Three Generations of Photographers

The science of photography was 32 years old when Alexander Johnston took an interest in it in 1861. Niépie had taken the first acknowledged photograph in France in 1828 using a long involved process which is almost unrecognisable as photography today. In fact one of the reasons for the slow progress of this technological marvel was that the pioneers required considerable scientific training and background. As such, interest and research into it was confined to a handful of people with the necessary skills. But as in many scientific fields, processes were improved and simplified and gradually attracted the interest of more and more people. And there seems to be a strange thread connecting Alexander Johnston to the evolution of photography. Niépie produced his first photograph the year before his father, William Johnston, a plumber, was sent in 1829 by his employers, Charles Coventry of Edinburgh, to fit the lead sheet flashing to the roof of the new Wick Parish Kirk. William Johnston belonged to Prestonpans and had gone to Edinburgh to serve his apprenticeship with a firm of Charles Coventry. He seems to have enjoyed a close relationship with his employer as one of his children was called after him. When his work on the roof was completed in 1830 he decided to stay in the rapidly expanding town which seemed to offer good opportunities to the ambitious young plumber who wanted to set up his own business.

He married Louisa Williamson, daughter of a local cabinet maker and they had five children, Charles, James, David, Alexander and Louisa. Alexander was born on 29th April, 1839, in Shore Lane, Wick, very shortly after William Henry Fox Talbot perfected his paper negative which meant that photographs could be reproduced merely by printing from the negative as opposed to the previous process of repeatedly taking the picture. In 1843, the year before he went to school, the world-famous partnership of Octavius Hill and Robert Adamson was formed in Edinburgh to photograph the ministers who had formed the Free Church in Scotland.

In 1851 when he was 12, two events took place which revolutionised photography. Scott Archer introduced the glass negative coated with collodion, and the Crystal Palace Exhibition of that year was held to promote science and new discoveries. While it is largely a matter of conjecture regarding the effect they may have had on their return, it is a fact that the Wick distilling family of Henderson attended the exhibition and must have talked of what they saw on their return home. Whether this had any influence on young Alexander Johnston, whose father they would certainly have known, is uncertain, but he left school in 1853 to join his father and brother Charles in business. He does not seem to have served his time as a plumber but was more of a book-keeper to the expanding business. At one time he worked for a spell as a clerk at Wick Harbour where he picked up a smattering of foreign languages, particularly Norwegian. However, he returned to the family firm and by 1859 or so his interest in photography was beginning to awaken.

In 1863 he had sufficient confidence in his ability to set up a studio behind the plumber's shop which was near Parliament Square in Wick. It seems to have taken him some time to build up the business and his activities were mostly confined to harbour and general scenes with only a little in the way of posed portraiture. He used the wet plate process which required a considerable knowledge of chemicals and involved the use of a small mobile darkroom, which he pushed around on a hand cart. In this, behind a screen to exclude light, he had to feel in the dark to find the appropriate chemicals and pour then on the plates as the process required.

However, photography was beginning to catch the public imagination and by 1869 or 1870 he had to move to larger premises in Bridge Street as people began to come to him, and his brother James who worked with him, to have their photographs taken. Between 1870 and the outbreak of the First World War the firm was to take about 60,000 portraits of individuals, families, friends, workmates and weddings.

In 1869, Alexander went in the carriage with Mr D. R. Simpson, a local ironmonger, to photograph the miners in the Kildonan gold fields, a journey which took them four days. As the demand for individual photographs grew, they became very heavily committed to this but still found time to photograph many outdoor events and street scenes. Alexander married Annie Cormack, daughter of a local fishcurer and they had five children, William, Annie, John, Louisa and Alexander. William, who was to follow his father and uncle into the business was born in Millers Square, Wick, on 25th October, 1879. The business continued to grow and was unchecked by Alexander's sudden death in 1896, in Edinburgh, where he had gone for medical treatment. At the age of 17, William had to assume partnership with his uncle and travelled daily to Thurso on the train to take photographs as they had by now opened a branch there. The plumbing side of the concern was now being run by his cousin Jimmy Johnston, and it ceased with his death in 1918.

His uncle James died in 1908 and William assumed sole responsibility for the business on the photographic side from that year. Many innovations had been made during this time, both in the methods of taking and processing photographs. The introduction of the roll film by George Eastman had now put photography within reach of the masses who would, in the fullness of time, start using mass produced cameras to take their own photographs. It was not until after the First World War that this really gathered momentum and William, who was a very progressive man, changed with the times and began processing the films for the local chemists nad other customers. There was still a demand of course for the traditional kind of photography and William took many hundreds of pictures of the events in and around the town, and further afield, where he photographed many country scenes and villages. In his youth he had even cycled the 17 miles to John O'Groats to capture the start of an early automobile race. When his son Alexander returned to Wick from Art College in 1932, he joined his father and made the daily train journey to Thurso to maintain their interests there. But times were changing and the Thurso studio was closed in 1938. Alexander was recruited to the Air Force as a photographer in 1941 and was to remain in the services for the next 4½ years. On his return to civilian life he resumed his position with his father until the latter's death in 1950.

He continued the business on his own behalf until he retired in 1975. Thus ended an era of 112 years of photography by the one family. Between them the Johnstons took almost 100,000 photographs.

Alexander Johnston's original studio in Wick.

Foreword

This book was originally intended to introduce the work of the Johnston family of photographers to an audience who may not have been aware of the contribution that they had made to Scottish photography. As the text developed the character of the work changed to become a history of Wick harbour, illustrated by the priceless photographs taken by the Johnstons. It is not intended to provide the details of how the herring industry functioned at its basic structure, either in Wick or elsewhere. The practices were universal.

There are many excellent books on the subject and they explain fully how the organisation worked in respect of all the trades that were involved. This book, as it evolved, is only intended to make the works of the Johnston family, and the general history of the herring fishing in Wick, available to readers who may not be informed on these subjects. The restrictions of space and time have limited the contents of the book to a small part of both the photographs and text that are available. Of necessity a great deal of subject matter must remain either in the negative collection of the Wick Society or in the notes of the author.

But for the following people, many of whom patiently sat with me and recorded their recollections, sometimes for hours on end, a great deal of detail would have been impossible to obtain. Many have passed away since I made the recordings with them, but I will always be in their debt.

They are: Skipper William Thain of the 'Zoe,' Wick.
Skipper Jim Bremner of the 'Fisher Boy,' Wick.
Skipper Donald Miller of the 'Spindrift,' Wick.
Skipper Rab More of the 'Alert,' Wick.
Mr David Stewart of the 'Whiteheather,' Wick.
Mr Angus MacDonald, pilot, Wick.
Mr Alex Mowat, crofter fisherman, John O'Groats.
Mr David Simpson, seaman, Stroma.
Mr George Mackay, ice manufacturer, Staxigoe.
Mr Adam Hendry, farmer, Wick
Mr Alex Matheson, carter, Wick
Mr John Swanson, foreman cooper, Wick.
Mr John Gunn, cooper, Wick.
Mr William Sinclair, Wick Harbour Trust.
Mr David Simpson, ironmonger, Wick.

There were three others, who had died before I had the use of a tape recorder, but they lit a spark in me when I first used to visit them as they mended the "Fisher Boy's" nets when I was a young boy. They were my grandfather, Jim Baikie, and his lifelong companions, Jock Bremner and Neil Stewart.

I trust that they have found a quiet anchorage in sheltered waters.

Iain Sutherland,
Wick.

Wick Harbour and the Herring Fishing

Fishing from boats has been pursued from Wick since Viking times. No one can say with confidence when exactly it began and it could well have been conducted by the Catti, the tribes who lived here before the Vikings arrived. The Romans recorded in the year 240 that the people of the Hebrides lived on a great deal of fish and it is probably a safe assumption that the people living on the seaboard of Caithness did likewise. Very little evidence has been found to support this theory but very many limpet shells have been recovered from their dwellings and it is reasonable to conclude that they caught fish as well. Exactly how, or if they did so, must remain a matter of conjecture but evidence from excavations at Freswick show beyond doubt that the Vikings landed fish on the Caithness coast in very large quantities. These bones were of the larger cod, haddock and whiting with no trace of herring, possibly because the fishing methods of these days were designed to catch the larger, deeper swimming fish.

So we cannot say with certainty when the herring fishing began, but as in all human pursuits which stretch back through the ever thickening mists of time, there are significant events, dates and people, standing as milestones to direct the traveller of history's highways and byeways. Of course the closer these milestones stand to the present day, the more clearly they record the details and the more information they give.

And like the evolution of so many other industries, in so many other places, the Caithness herring fishery grew as a result of many influences, both internal and external. The internal reactions were the abilities of local men to take advantage of the conditions which the external influences created to allow them to exploit their great natural resource, the herring. The drive which was to achieve the success was a local one but the impetus which gave this drive its momentum was not. As in the decline of the industry, its success was a response to these outside influences.

The Caithness coast, like many others around the coast of Europe, sits at certain times of year in what is literally a sea of herring. Many countries of Europe, according to the whim of nature, over the centuries, flourished or foundered according to whether the migrating shoals of herring visited their coasts or not. Many accepted whatever fate befell them and poverty, starvation, and racial extinction even, overcame them with the disappearance of the herring from their coasts. Others were more resilient and sent their fleets abroad to follow the shoals, or locate new grounds and as the 13th, 14th and 15th centuries followed one another the whole North Sea, or German Ocean as it was called, became the hunting ground for the European fleets. For hundreds of years, long before the Caithness men shared in the harvest, the Dutch, Flemings, Fresians, French, English, Belgians, Danes, Germans and on the fringes, the Scots. Untold riches were drawn from the North Sea in general and the Scottish waters in particular. Many wars were fought between the contending nations as each sought to apply a permanent claim to the fishing grounds, representing as they did wealth and freedom from starvation. It was quite common for the warships of one country to sink all the fishing fleet of another if they happened to come across them. This of course brought retaliation and in the 15th and 16th centuries fishing fleets had to sail in convoys protected by their battleships. Such was the importance of herring, not least among its attraction being the fact that, when in barrels, it provided a very convenient form of food for the many armies which fought and refought their ways across Europe.

Yet one of the great ironies of the time, all through this period of history, was that the Scots only played a very minor part and benefited least. Although these huge shoals could be found from Shetland, down past both the east and west coasts, and beyond into English waters, the Scots could never get themselves organised to take part properly. There were many reasons for this.

It was not that the Scots were unaware of the shoals. Far from it. It was just that they were never able to disentangle themselves from other, greater, problems long enough to realise the full potential offered by the herring. The irony is even greater when one considers that Scotland, probably the most impoverished country in Europe at the time, was sitting on this wealth and could do very little about it.

The harbour 1860's full of Scaffies. Second class boats carried the numbers before the letters in the registration number e.g. 132 WK.

The most important reasons why the Scots could never become involved as they would have liked were geographical and political. For three centuries Scotland waged incessant wars with England and the few fishing ports that it did have, were all around the Firths of Forth and Tay, within easy reach of marauding English armies. The struggle to resist these invaders occupied the civil administrations almost totally as they struggled to rebuild the economy which was being destroyed with almost monotonous regularity. If that was not enough, there was the long lasting civil strife and rivalry between the ruling classes who were continuously plotting to overthrow or obstruct each other. Add to this the total lack of roads, communications and the fact that north of Perth the Highland chiefs were a law unto themselves who frequently were in a state of open rebellion, it is hardly to be wondered at that the fishing industry never really got on a proper footing unil hundreds of years passed. Till then they could only stand impotently by and watch while other nations gathered the harvest of their seas.

This impotence was intensified by the fact that the Scots were fully aware that the herring could be the saving of their country if they could only get peace enough to catch them. Once, out of sheer frustration they even declared war on Dutch fishing vessels, and it was six years before things settled down again. This time, 1410, it should be mentioned, was one of the rare occasions on which the Scots had a warship.

As early as 1138, in the reign of David I, concessions were being granted in respect of herring fishing and during the following five centuries the Scots Parliament, when their minds were not diverted by other, more pressing problems, passed law upon law aimed at controlling and promoting the catching of herring. They tried to cover everything and, during the periods of comparative peace with England, actually managed to get some of them enforced. Not on the foreign vessels, with the notable exception of their attacks on the Dutch, but did manage to foster the fishings in the Firth of

Scaffies lined up at the harbours on the north side of the bay in 1864.

Forth now and again. The detail is too great to illustrate here but briefly: laws were passed to regulate the size of nets, close seasons, the sizes of the barrels, which varied from port to port, the size of the boats, working conditions, pay, tax relief, and the kind of salt to be used. Barrels had to be marked with the name of the curer and the cooper so that any defaulter could be identified. Officers were appointed to inspect the quality of the fish for export as the parliament realised that a high quality product would be good for the country's reputation. Even the potential of the industry as a source of taxation and jobs was not overlooked and as early as 1240 a value added tax was introduced on a last, or 10,000 herrings. In 1491 the unemployed were order to find work at the sea or be driven from the towns. A Job Creation Scheme backfired, as it effectively turned the unemployed into bonded slaves. Other laws, in response to pressure from the Royal Burghs, one of the three component parts of the Scots Parliament, or Three Estates as it was known, were passed which said that fish could only be landed at Royal Burghs. It took 100 years to correct this error which destroyed the economies of the towns which were not Royal Burghs. A fishing limit for foreign vessels of 17 miles, which the country could never enforce, was introduced in 1491 and this and all the other laws lay on the statute books until the union of the crowns of Scotland and England in 1603. It was only after this time that peace between the countries finally became a reality and the previous legislation had a chance of lasting success.

Scotland of course retained its Parliament until 1707 and until that time it functioned quite independently of the English Parliament. It was during these 104 years that the glimmering of the legislation, which was to have such an incredible effect on Caithness, and many other places, began to shine through the mirk of the frustration of the previous centuries.

The first step, as a precursor to the Union of the Crowns, was taken in 1602 when Scotland and

Coopers in the Johnston Studio.

A posed photograph of coopers with the tools of their trade in the 1860's.

Fishermen posed in Johnston studio in 1860's.

In the Johnston Studio.

How the elements can reduce an elegant vessel.

England agreed on a fishing limit of 14 miles. The difference this time was that the Scots had the English fleet, the most powerful in Europe, to back it up. But it was not till 1661 that an idea, which in 127 years was to give birth to its illustrious descendant, the British Fisheries Society, was first turned to law. On 1st January an Act was passed to encourage the establishment of a fishing company to set up fishing stations around the coasts. An incentive to it was the fact that the materials they used would be exempt from taxation. It had the disadvantage of barring the sale of herring on the domestic market by people who were not members of the companies, creating in effect a monopoly for the monied sections of the community as the vast majority of the population was totally unable to subscribe the capital. Although the activities were restricted to a few people, they achieved great success and it was realised that if the concessions could be extended then more people could become involved and hence more wealth generated. Attempts at more widely based legislation were frustrated by the company, as they saw their privileged positions being threatened. But in 1690 the Act setting up the Company was repealed, mainly because the Company had sub-let its franchise to other people and had ceased to promote fishing itself, merely drawing on the tax concessions, or refunds, for which it had originally qualified. But the legislation was beginning to come good, as far as the promotion of the industry was concerned, because in this Act a drawback, or refund of tax, was extended to all who exported herring. While this still did not put the common man directly in touch with the opportunities offered it did begin to widen the scope for enterprising men with the acumen to see the potential. There were difficulties in the payment of this refund and in 1698 the customs officers were made responsible for paying this refund which was £10.45 Scots money on every last, or 10,000 herrings exported. And the merchant could take them to court if they delayed payment.

View over Donald Reid's harbour, one of the six small harbours which were on the north side of the bay. The North river jetty runs ashore.

The ill-fated breakwater under construction about 1866. A miniature locomotive is pulling the bogeys used to transport the stone from the South Head Quarries.

This is a painting made before photographs could be taken successfully at night. Light was supplied by wadding torches.

The industry was given a boost in 1702 when the French attacked and sank 400 Dutch fishing boats off Bressay, effectively destroying the Dutch fishing industry for a century. But the expansion was still very slow, mainly due to the fact that herring fishing was conducted by a type of ship called a buss, a sort of mother ship which fished with smaller boats and processed their catches. And the cost of these ships was only within the resources of a few. This, along with the restrictive practices which only allowed herring to be landed at certain ports, extracted heavy landing dues, various forms of levies, prevented a rapid exploitation of the misfortunes which befel the Dutch. One of the most damaging restrictions was the law that said that only foreign salt could be used for curing because the import of salt was in the hands of a monopoly which had great parliamentary influence.

But progress was being made, albeit painfully slowly, and in 1727 a Board of Trustees was set up to promote the fishing industry. And one of the powers they were given was the ability to reward fishermen who discovered herring shoals around the coast. Although comparatively unimportant in its way it was the information sent in by these fishermen which finally established the enormous extent of the herring shoals around the coasts. The Board of Trustees seems to have done very little with the information and the industry was left to its own devices for another 25 years. Another attempt to set up an organisation was made in 1750, to form yet another company, but that failed miserably due mainly to the fact that those who subscribed the capital knew nothing about the herring industry. The Act also provided for a bounty to be paid of 30 shillings a ton for all vessels fitted out for the herring **fishing of between 20 and 80 tons. In 1756 the legislators finally, just about, made the regulations** which would trigger off the massive growth in the herring fishing during the following century. They enacted that fishermen could have free use of any harbour, shore, lochs or creek for landing fish, curing, drying nets or any other lawful pursuit of their trade. Now although fishermen could not afford to build the large busses to fish, they could negotiate a share of the bounty on exported herring with the curers, in their own locality, where they could land herring on any suitable shore. The stage had finally, after 500 years, been set.

Waiting for room 1864.

A few irregularities were ironed out in 1757 and the bounty was increased to 50 shillings a ton for the busses. Net regulations were relaxed and gradually the effects spread.

The first Caithness man to take advantage of the new opportunities did not do so until 1767, which may be identified as the first milestone in the history of the Caithness Fishing. He was Alexander Miller, of the Field Farm in Staxigoe, two miles north of Wick, who, in conjunction with his partners John Anderson and John Sutherland sent a boat from Staxigoe to fish for herring under the export bounty scheme. Their first year of operation was marred by the non-payment of these bounties as this could have serious consequences where a man could not offset the tax paid on the materials he used. As it was the men were of sufficient capital to wait till the following year, 1768, for the payment. However, the lessons, and advantages of the system were not lost on their neighbours. By 1790 over 150 boats, both local and from the south side of the Moray Firth, were fishing off the coast during the summer season, which lasted from June to nearly October. There were no harbours of any description and the boats operated from suitable rock faces or beaches. The start made by Miller, who was to become a very wealthy man, soon spread to the surrounding inlets of Greenigoe, Ottersgoe, Broadhaven and Ramsigoe which lay between Staxigoe and Wick Bay. Although Wick was a burgh of great antiquity it did not have a harbour as such — only a rough quay as most of the small trade it had was taken over the then sandy shores of its river.

And by 1790 two events had taken place which finally opened the door wide to the opportunities which lay beyond. The fishing in Caithness was conducted from small open boats and was slowly growing while elsewhere in Scotland the number of herring busses was falling. This had largely been due to the inability of the administrators to pay the bounty and to wrangles over the size of the vessels and consequently the amount of bounty to be paid. The first of these events came in 1785 when it was decreed that the bounty could be paid either on the boat or the herring it caught. In the previous years the Exchequer had profited by the increased revenues being paid by men who were trying to qualify for the bounty by buying boats and materials and they realised that the way to increase the taxation

A schooner running the bay on a very stormy day.

returns would be to allow more people access to the fishing. The direct subsidy on the barrel of herring was the answer, as it encouraged men with not enough capital for the purchase of a buss to fish from smaller boats, as Miller had anticipated.

The problem of the lack of harbours, facilities and capital was solved the following year, 1786, by the institution of The British Society for Extending the Fisheries and Improving the Sea Coasts of the Kingdom, later to be known as the British Fisheries Society. This body was charged with the responsibility of overall control of the expansion of the fishing industry by building villages, harbours and roads and, most importantly, to make finance available at low interest rates to fishermen or others who wished to progress in life. And their greatest achievement, among many outstanding successes, was to be the creation of the village of Pulteneytown just across the river from the Royal Burgh of Wick.

The connection between the then empty land, save 9 crofters, and the Society began in earnest on 6th August, 1792, when John Rennie one of the Society's surveyors arrived in Wick to write his report on the possibility of building a harbour and village on the lands offered to the Society by Sir Benjamin Dunbar, proprietor of the estate of Hempriggs. He estimated the cost of the harbour, designed to hold 300 vessels at £14,441 9 shillings. It was to be 10 years before his superior, the great Thomas Telford, chief engineer to the Society came to Wick to give final approval to the scheme and he sought Treasury approval to proceed on 25th May of that year. The plan was for a village of 1000 people, with all the yards, stores and buildings required to support them. He suggested that the village be called Pulteneytown in honour of Sir William Pulteney, Chairman of the Society.

In 1802 Caithness was a very isolated community and had very little contact with the rest of the country. There were no roads and the only communication with the south was either by sea or by horseback. The population was about 17,000 and Wick itself was more of a township with only two main streets and 600 inhabitants. Apart from Thurso, which was of comparable size, the rest of the county's population lived in hamlets or on small holdings where they eked out a living that just held body and soul together. But already a few of these hamlets on the coast were showing, as was Wick, signs of stirring into life in pursuit of the herring. The most notable of these was Staxigoe which, until the construction of Pulteneytown harbour, maintained a position of pre-eminence.

Construction of the harbour began in 1803 and proceeded slowly in the beginning, mainly due to the shortage of skilled masons, blacksmiths and other trades which were not available locally. But these difficulties were solved as more people came to the town and the local people learned the appropriate trades. And one of these was James Bremner, to become world famous for his prowess as an engineer.

He was born in 1784 at Keiss, north of Wick, and had served his time as a ship's carpenter in Greenock, returning to Caithness in 1805, just in time to be involved with the construction of the harbour almost from the very beginning. Although he had his own shipbuilding, repairing and quarrying companies in the new village he worked as consultant for the Society, in many of their enterprises elsewhere. He was a man of enormous talents and kindliness and all his contemporaries spoke warmly of him. In the future he was to become one of the most successful salvers of sunken and wrecked ships. He recovered over 300 of them during his lifetime among which, in 1847, was the steamship 'Great Britain' after Brunel had failed to refloat her.

But in the early 1800's he was occupied with establishing his shipbuilding yard and subcontracting for George Burn the master of the new harbour works, which were completed in 1811. Telford meantime had completed his design for the new town, the only one he was ever to create from start to finish, and construction work was proceeding apace on the area known as Lower Pulteneytown. The first of the yards were being let and in 1807 the first tea shop, originally for meeting the demands of the construction force, was opened. By 1813 there were over 300 inhabitants in an area where 14 years before there had been about 15, and the population passed 1000 in 1816.

A Scaffie to the gunwhales with herring c1870.

The north side of Wick River showing the old swing bridge which was demolished in 1936.

The curing station and cooperages at the Black Rock which were operated by 2 Fraserburgh firms, Donaldson and Bruce. The old harbour of Port Dunbar, earlier known as Donald Reid's harbour is in the foreground.

When not at work the gutters were as smartly dressed as anybody.

This photograph seems to have been taken very early or very late in the season from the quantity of boats which are hauled on the quay. Among those in the water are the Christina of Lybster, WK.420, the Catherine and Helen of Lybster WK.796 and the Fisher Lassie of Helmsdale WK.195.

2 Scaffies in harbour mouth. One with a new sail and the other being pushed out with wands.

An unidentified schooner dressed overall. She is flying the Norwegian flag.

Part of the giant squid which caused rumours of sea monsters when it was washed ashore at Ackergill.

The fishing fleet had grown in proportion and the harbour was overcrowded to the extent that it frequently became paralysed. Apart from the difficulties experienced with the press of vessels trying to use it, both fishing and cargo boats, the harbour entrance was continually silting up very badly. Even with the highest tides there was only 13 ft of water at best and at low water it was impossible for any but the smallest boats to use the harbour. Shipmasters reverted to loading and unloading their vessels in the bay, using barges with oar power only, to ferry the cargoes ashore rather than risk being trapped for what could be weeks in the harbour. The process was very expensive, as the barges had to be hired and much injury was done to life and limb when the cargoes were being handled under difficult sea conditions. Eventually, concluding that they were no worse off using ports which had no harbours, such as Broadhaven and Greenigoe, the shipowners threatened to take their trade there unless something was done about it.

The Society, who administered the village of Pulteneytown quite independently of the Wick Town Council, responded, although they were probably planning an extension to the harbour anyway. By 1820 plans were being studied and in 1824 an extension, by way of the construction of a new harbour basin was authorised. The work began in 1826, under the charge of James Bremner and, as events proved, the extension was sorely needed.

About 600 boats were coming to the summer fishings now and the resident population of 1500 was being augmented by an influx of 4000 visitors during the season. Many of these, and their numbers were to increase in the next 30 years, were the victims of the Highland Clearances which were beginning to gather momentum in the counties of Sutherland, Ross and Inverness. Pulteneytown

An auction of large cod in the 1890's. By the turn of the century the cod were laid in rows with every 20th having its head laid to the tail of its neighbours to indicate a score, the selling unit.

offered the prospect of work and consequently some kind of relief from the deprivation which they suffered. Many of these people, whose only language was Gaelic, walked across the hills to the town, a journey of well over 100 miles which could take a week or more to complete. The extension to the harbour, involving as it did the closure of the original entrance and the opening of another in deeper water, took 4 years and cost £20,000. Of this £5000 had been incurred in repairing the damage done to the works by a storm on 20th September, 1827 which demolished most of the works done to that date. However, the completion of the harbour extension signalled the beginning of the most successful era in the history of Pulteneytown and as a result of its construction trade expanded unchecked for the next 40 years.

The town grew in all directions, both physically and industrially. And as it grew so the influence of the British Fisheries Society declined over its affairs.

From the beginning of the construction, the Society had administered Pulteneytown from its London offices, originally, through a resident agent in the burgh but as the success of the venture grew apace this became more and more difficult. The slow and irregular communication of the early days had been improved with the opening of the highway to the south in 1816. But the ever increasing volume, and complexity of the decision-making created a wide variety of problems. A variety which in the fullness of time proved too much both for the agent and the Board, who were hundreds of miles away. Even with modern communications this would prove a very difficult task and the fact that the Society succeeded in administering the Burgh for so long speaks highly of the calibre of the men who carried the responsibilities. By 1830 the resident population of the town had risen to nearly

A ten barrel cart used exclusively in the herring trade.

2,300, a number which was augmented during the summer by about six to seven thousand visitors. The languages of at least 10 European countries could be heard on the streets any day. Dialects from all the fishing ports of Scotland lay on the tongues of many of the visitors, and three thousand of the migrants spoke only Gaelic.

Everything was expanding in all directions. The new parish Kirk had been completed in 1830 and the timbers for the roof were so large that they had to be floated up river as they could not be taken through the narrow streets on the north side of the river. They had been imported from Russia in the Wick schooner 'Bittern' under the command of Captain Donald Munro, just about the same time as a young plumber, William Johnston, came to Wick to put the lead flashings on the roof for which these enormous baulks of Russian timbers were destined.

The expansion of the town during this period, and in the times to follow, brought with it social conditions which fell far short of those that are considered acceptable in the late 20th century. The most urgent during the summer was accommodation as the town had to find temporary lodgings for its visitors who outnumbered the residents by nearly three to one. This problem was also shared by the surrounding villages such as Staxigoe, Broadhaven, Sarclet, which had boomed along with Wick, but not of course to the same degree. People lodged wherever they could, in cellars, garrets, sail lofts, barns, sheds and in dormitories which had been built above the curing yards to accommodate the thousands of lassies who came to gut the herring. And of course such overcrowding, which was to get worse as the fishing continued to grow, brought in its wake the inevitable spate of contagious diseases. Outbreaks of cholera, typhus and diptheria were quite common and between 1833 and 1834 cholera was so prevalent along the coast that many visitors stayed away and the fishings were put into check for three years. It was not till 1846 when piped water reached the harbour that there was any decrease in the regularity of these outbreaks, which still occurred sporadically even after that date, although not on the scale seen previously.

It was during this period, up to the retiral of James Bremner from business, that the town achieved self sufficiency in almost all its needs. The distillery had been opened in 1827 and by 1844

Shaltigoe before the lifeboat station was built there. The rump of the ill-fated breakwater is visible in the distance. The curing yards are James More, Davidsons and Calders.

over 800 gallons of whisky a week were being consumed in the summer season in the 44 licensed premises which were concentrated mainly in the harbour area. Bremner was building the schooners it needed and a dozen smaller yards were building the fishing boats. It had a brewery, sail manufacturers, ropeworks, foundries, cooperages, saw mills, net works, furniture manufacturers, although the greatest of these, McEwans did not begin operation till the 1850's, and a dozen other trades. Social life was equally hectic with dances, concerts, plays, soirées, travelling shows, ceilidhs, debating societies, lectures and of course a very strong presence for the various denominations of the Church. At one time, from the 1840's to the 1860's Wick had the largest Gaelic speaking congregation of any church in the world. Over 1500 people would attend the services and prayer meetings which required 3 ministers at one time to officiate over them. And one of the features of the period was the very low crime rate. Until 1844 there was not even a police force in Pulteneytown and law and order does not seem to have been a great issue during these times when the town must have had all the appearance and activity of a boom town. The explanation may be in the fact that the population lived in very close quarters with one another and consequently everybody knew everybody else's business, but the main law-breaking seems to have been confined to brawling and petty theft.

But 1844 was another of the prominent dates in the progress of the fishing in Pulteneytown. For some years the prominent business men and ratepayers in the town had been expressing dissatisfaction with the administration of the town by the British Fisheries Society and had petitioned several times for the creation of a local body to run its affairs and the Pulteney Commissioners or an elected council, were established that year. They had no responsiblity for managing the harbour but had to see to the maintenance of the streets, the continuing expansion of the town, and other day to day matters concerned with running the Burgh. For their coat of arms they adopted a motif of circular design with three herring displayed on it against a background of a net.

A family redding and baiting the small lines. This photograph may have been taken in Sarclet, 3 miles south of Wick.

Drying Sails.

The schooner Elba, with hatch open, prepares to ship herring as an eight barrel cart stands ready on the quay.

The Society retained the responsibility for the operations at the harbour which again was proving inadequate. Great difficulties were being experienced with silting in the harbour mouth and great local pressures were being brought to bear on them to build yet more extensions. James Bremner was among their leading critics. He drew up plans for the construction of several basins, further out into the bay and, in support of his claims, forecast that the day was not far away when all coastal traffic would be carried by steam boats, for which the harbour in its present form was totally unsuitable. But the Society were having great financial difficulties because of the heavy drain placed on their funds by the maintenance of Pulteneytown harbour. An attempt to extend the harbour was to be made later, 20 years later, but that was some way ahead. The late forties saw continuous expansion and in 1848 disaster struck when 41 boats and 37 men were lost while trying to run the bay during a severe storm. As a result of this the government set up a Board of Enquiry under the chairmanship of Captain Washington to establish if anything could be done to reduce the very heavy loss of life incurred at sea. The Board published its report in 1849 and it made several sweeping recommendations, which were to have a far reaching effect on both Pulteneytown and its surrounding villages. The most important recommendation that it made was that more decked vessels should be built, a proposal that was stronly resisted at first, and among the ranks of the critics of the Report was no less a personage than James Bremner himself. He and the others argued that a decked boat was not necessarily safer, as the Washington Report concluded, than a decked boat. It would be twice as heavy and twice as expensive.

c1900. There were 3 companies curing here James More, Davidson of Leith and Joseph Calder. The salmon station, with drying nets in the foreground was operated by A. Buchan.

Hauling nets in the morning c1890.

Schooners and fishing boats drying their sails. The Fifie Oaktree, beneath the bows of the Euphemia on the left, has her port of registration, Portknockie and her skippers name, Mair, on her starboard quarter. This was quite a common practice.

Running for the harbour, well reefed down in a half gale.

A Stornoway Fifie follows the First, WK.1, under a threatening sky.

Two minutes later WK.1, the First, has the safety of the harbour within reach. Schooners await the storm at anchor and under bare poles out in the deep water.

A pipe shank drifter, a conventional drifter, a converted sail boat and a sailing Zulu off the quay heads. The Zulu is taking in the S.E. wind.

Just enough wind to hold the sail away from the mast.

The Content, the first steam drifter in Wick.

The Content tows the hull of the Elsay to be outfitted in the harbour.

The 'Peep o Day' the second steam drifter to arrive in Wick.

James More's yard with the paraffin flares lit at the approach of darkness. The lassies worked till the last herring was gutted and this photograph must have been taken in late autumn or winter.

3 smaller Fifies and a ketch at the harbour mouth.

Since the beginning of the century the basic style of the boat hulls around the Caithness, and many other coasts, had not changed. They were completely undecked, with no shelter at all. In the beginning these boats, 'Scaffies' as they were called, had been about 20 to 25 feet long but had grown to 45 and even 50 feet by 1850. The only fishermen who used a different style of hull were these of the Fife coast who had the famous 'Fifie' hull, many of which at the time of the Washington Report were half, if not fully decked.

One of the great advantages of the open boat, apart from the fact that it was very cheap, was that it could be very easily hauled up on a beach, as many of the lesser ports were, in bad weather. This was one of the reasons why Staxigoe and all the other little harbours, including the six which were along the north side of Wick Bay, flourished for so long in the shadow of Pulteneytown.

However as time passed the recommendations of the Washington Report came to be accepted and became among the factors which hastened the demise of the smaller ports.

In 1851 the size of the fleet in Wick passed 1000 vessels for the first time and it was to remain over this number till 1862 when it reached its maximum of 1120. As with the fishing fleet, on shore commerce expanded rapidly as the town set up the supporting services which the trade required.

Facing work being carried out to the quay as the boats dry their sails.

There were now ship brokers, agents, vice consuls for the foreign countries, insurance agencies and commission agents. The shipping fleet was continuing to expand and Captain Cormack, the harbour-master had four sons who in their turn were captains of their own vessels. Alec of the ' Alert,' James of the ' Alma,' William of the 'Gem' and John of the ' Iona.' John was later to be drowned in 1876 while trying to rescue the crew of a German ship which went ashore in Sinclair Bay during a storm.

It was also at this time that three Wick schooners ' Rambler,' 'Stemster' and 'Gleaner' all left on the same day for Russia. All vanished and it would be many years before Wick shipowners would have vessels with names which ended in ' er.'

By the time of James Bremner's death in 1856 Wick had two weekly newspapers, the *John O'Groat Journal* founded in 1836, and the *Northern Ensign* established in 1851. There was moderate rivalry between them for the first few years of the *Ensign's* existence but in 1859 large scale riots broke out between the Highland visitors and the local fishermen. By that time the resident population was about 5000 and there was an annual influx of about 12,000 people, of which 4500 were from the Highlands and Islands. Although the fighting was confined to comparatively small numbers the Wick Town Council and the Pulteney Commissioners did not think that the Pulteney police force, of three men, and in whose jurisdiction most of the trouble occurred, would be able to control the trouble, even with the help of the six men of the Wick force and the 50 reserves that they had managed to muster. The army and navy were sent for, and in the event, the trouble fizzled out after 15 days. But the local papers feuded for a long time after the event as one, the *John O'Groat Journal* had been advocating a very firm hand, while the *Ensign* preached moderation.

Lassies touring the coastguard station during a weekend.

The Shaltigoe yards tidied away for the weekend.

Large unidentified steam ship ashore in Reiss Bay, 8 miles north of Wick.

Old boats used as sheds. This picture is either at Ackergill or John O'Groats.

A large Scaffie on the left, a Keiss Fifie in the middle and a Zulu from Findochty behind her. WK.208 is the Janets.

1862 was to see the largest fleet ever to use the harbour and it was to be the last year when the fleet was over 1000 vessels. In 2 days during that year the 3500 fisher lassies gutted 50 million herring and the pressures were building up on the British Fisheries Society to build a harbour of refuge to off-set some of the heavy loss of life and boats which continued remorselessly. The Society decided to go ahead with a scheme for a breakwater in Wick Bay at the then enormous cost of £100,000. Work began on 1st October, 1863, under the supervision of Robert Louis Stevenson's father, Thomas, of the famous firm of lighthouse builders.

Robert Louis himself stayed in Wick during this time and the enterprise was a disaster from start to finish, representing the only failure that this company was ever to experience in all its undertakings. 200 feet of the works were demolished by a storm on 21st December, 1868; it was replaced and another 400 feet was destroyed on 10th February, 1870. Another section was destroyed in 1872 and by 1873 the Society had had enough and its engineers declared the construction to be a ruin and abandoned it. All the money had been lost and this was a blow which knocked the heart completely out of the Board of the British Fisheries Society. Local pressure mounted to have control of the harbour passed into local hands and in 1879 an Act was passed by parliament giving control to Wick Harbour Trust, which held its inaugural meeting on 29th January, 1880.

But other events were taking place at the same time, not the least of which were the signs that many of the recommendation of the Washington Report were being implemented. And the most important of these had been the introduction of decking to the fishing boats. It took to about 1860, 11

The North of Scotland Steam Ship Company vessel St Ola at the quay heads in Wick. Her captain was 'Bonnie Willie' Swanson.

The yard in the foreground on the north side of the river belonged to D. Waters and Son, a company who also had a yard in Lower Pulteneytown.

The Paragon WK.712 wrecked on the north side of the bay. She was one of the largest boats to belong to the Island of Stroma.

years after the Report was first issued. Originally the open 'Scaffie' boats were fitted with a half deck, forward, which provided a rough cabin for the men to sleep in while at sea during the night. The introduction of this shelter came about at the same time as Garibaldi was fighting the Italian Wars of Independence and the hull type became known as a 'Baldie.' It was soon realised that the shelter deck gave more protection and that the boats could get to sea in weather that would have not been considered earlier. Not only that but the addition of the deck offered opportunities to increase the size of the hulls and it was not long before full decking came into fashion.

Up to this time all herring nets had been made of hemp but cotton, which was ⅓ the weight, was introduced as a substitute in the early sixties and proved an immediate success. The boats were becoming larger and their catching power was increased dramatically as they could now carry more nets, which in turn gave rise to a larger boat and consequently a bigger crew. The twenty years following 1860 saw a complete revolution in the industry.

Experiments with steam fishing boats were now being conducted as the increase in size allowed enough room to install engines; but it was to be 20 years yet before Wick had a steam drifter. And other experiments were taking place. On 7th December, 1879 at Asher's Yard in Burghead, a boat called the 'Nonesuch' was launched. This was an entirely new design of hull which contained the best features of the old 'Scaffie' and 'Fifie' hulls. As the wars against the Zulu chieftain Cetawayo were being fought at the time, she was dubbed a 'Zulu.' This hull type never received much popularity in

The schooner 'Hans' of Sweden ashore at Broadhaven.

Wick and none were built there although a few were later bought into the port. The Wick fishermen preferred to stick to the ' Scaffie,' and increasingly the 'Fifie' type hulls for their sailing vessels.

The size of the fleet began to diminish from 1863 although its catch remained constant for the next 50 years. And the signs of the decline in the neighbouring villages were becoming visible as the more progressive skippers who had invested in the larger boats had no alternative but to bring them to Wick for a safe mooring. It was imperceptible at first but the slide to extinction had begun. In 1888 Wick still had 530 boats and 46 schooners and smacks on the register but there were also increasing signs that the Continental customers were beginning to use their own much larger steam ships to convey their herring. And the most important reason for this was that freight charges could be cut dramatically by using vessels which could carry ten times as much herring as the local schooners. And they also had the capacity to visit other ports, such as Stornoway or Lerwick to make up their cargoes if necessary, thus effectively cutting out, each one, the need for 10 small schooners.

Yet another factor as far as freight was concerned was the opening of the railway in 1875 and many cargoes which previously went by sea, now travelled by this method. As indeed did the workers who, a few years later, were to leave the town for the fishings in Yarmouth after the Wick season finished. But all of this had a gradual effect and the long term results were not at all apparent except to the most astute.

The St Nicolas ashore on Proudfoot. She was a total loss.

The guts from the herring were sold to farmers for manure. Nothing was wasted.

The Sillarsburn Curing Stations on the north side of the river. In the foreground is Tom Murray's station on the quay between the very small Sandison's harbour and Mowat's harbour, neither of which are visible in the picture.

The Wick schooner 'Flown' just arrived home from the continent.

A heavily laden Scaffie in the foreground. WK.204 is the Maggie of Lybster.

Launch of the Chance from Messrs Alexander's yard. WK.434 is hauled on the quay in the background.

The Ella taking on coal at the north quay.

Waiting for the tide 1930s.

Steam Drifters landing herring in front of the power station with BF.249 Valar Crown in the foreground. She was a regular visitor to Wick for very many years.

In the early 1860's some experiments had been conducted, mainly in the English ports of Hull, Grimsby and Brixham, with a new concept in fishing called trawling. The herring fishermen reacted with anger and aggression to the men who employed this method because the trawling was conducted over many of the herring spawning grounds. Indeed in the early days the ropes, which towed the trawl across the bottom, were often so covered with the sticky herring spawn that the crews of the trawlers had great difficulty in hauling them. The herring fishermen, one of whose champions was Mr Vansittart Coneybeare, conducted a long campaign over the next 20 years to have this method of fishing banned in inshore waters.

Meetings were held up and down the country, attended by hundreds of fishermen, demanding that trawling, which was becoming more efficient with the introduction of steam, be outlawed. The purpose of the meetings was to indicate to the government that public opinion was set against trawler men and many incidents, often violent, took place. There were occasional riots and in May, 1884, a trawler was driven from Macduff Harbour with stones. But the trawlers were gradually edging their way north and very many complaints were received from the fishermen about the damage to their gear as the trawlers ploughed among them. The government passed the Sea Fisheries Act of 1883 which required offending trawler owners to pay compensation to fishermen who had lost nets and gear as a result of their activities. But as most of the evidence was on the bottom of the sea, very little came of the law.

Some of the fleet in the 1920s making smoke in preparation for the sea. Note the enormous masts of the converted sailing boats in the foreground.

The Sunbeam on her way between the new and old harbours.

BF.2042. The Bonnie Lass of Findochty follows the fleet out on a calm afternoon about 1900.

James More's yard, Shaltigoe.

The Chance after completion but before she had her registration number painted on.

The Wharf 1930's.

Loading barrels of herring at the north quay in Wick, regardless of what Mr Johnston wrote on his negative.

The Sunny Devon lands a large shot of herring.

YH.999, the Provider of Yarmouth and BF.1539 the Swallow of Buckie in the dry dock in 1913.

Drifters waiting for the tide to come in. Those in the harbour are aground.

Gutters in the 1930's. They not only gutted the herring but selected them into different grades at the same time.

A view across the harbour from the north side of Wick River taken in the 1920's.

The Elsay after completion.

James More's yard at Shaltigoe. One of the largest in the town.

Huuuuup!

The Pathfinder, an Orkney smack which was converted to a motor yacht by Messrs Alexander for the Harmsworth family.

The staff of George Cormack's yard in Lower Pulteneytown.

On 5th March, 1885, two trawlers, the 'Royal Duke' of Sunderland and the 'Miss Roberts' of Aberdeen landed fish in Wick. The local fishermen, some of whom received 30 days in prison for their pains, assaulted the crews, dumped the fish into the harbour, and even attacked the salesman who was trying to sell the fish. This incident went a long way to persuade interested parties that Aberdeen might be a better place to establish a base for the trawling industry. By the end of the century, in 1896, sufficient attention had been drawn to the desires of the herring fishermen that the Court of Session ruled that the Moray Firth should be closed to trawlers, under the Herring Fisheries Act of 1889. It was to remain closed to trawlers long after the herring fishing finally ceased.

Although the quantity of boats using the harbour during the close of the century was decreasing their size was increasing and congestion in the harbour was not any less than it had been 40 years previously. The boats were now reaching a size of sixty and even seventy feet in length and plans were drawn up for yet another harbour of refuge, this time to be built right at the mouth of the bay, with huge piers extending from the headlands on either side. The cost would be enormous but it had been suggested that the new prison which was going to be built in Scotland should be sited at Wick and the convict labour used to construct the new scheme, thus reducing the cost considerably. There was enormous public outcry in the town against the proposal for a prison and consequently it was decided to build it in Peterhead. Apart from the plans which are being deliberated upon in the 1980's, with one minor exception, this was the last serious attempt to solve the problems of the dangerous nature of the bay and harbour.

It was in the last ten years of the 19th century and the first 15 of the 20th that events, leading to the decline of the fishings began to gather speed, although, again, no one at the time would have recognised them as such. And Pulteneytown itself as a separate burgh would soon no longer exist.

A large Zulu which has been converted from sail to motor with a heavy catch well in excess of 100 crans.

In 1889 its police force, which had essentially been the private force of first the British Fisheries Society and then of the Commissioners, amalgamated with the county police force. As the century wore on there was increasing uncertainty about the ability of Pulteneytown to remain viable from the revenues that it was receiving from the rates and a campaign began to have it amalgamated with Wick. There was of course much opposition to the proposals.

On the face of it there was no need to amalgamate with Wick. With the notable exception of McEwans furniture factory nearly all the manufacturing effort was sited in Pulteneytown or just across the river on the north shore of the bay. The Distillery, nearly all the curing and associated yards were there. The ropeworks, the fish meal reduction plant, foundries, boat builders, engineers, railway, quarries, and above all, the harbour contributed to the economy. Wick by comparison had few fishcurers and the rest of its trade centred on service industries. But it did have the political pull of a Royal Burgh which had been in existence for 300 years and, at the end of the day it did not make a great deal of sense for an area with a total population of about 7000 to have two councils. So after 20 years of gradually mounting controversy the Pulteneytown Commissioners met for the last time on Monday, 25th February, 1902 with Provost Jamieson in the chair, and voted itself out of existence. On the 17th of March, the Scottish Office Provisional Order, Wick Burgh Extension was approved by Parliament and the burgh ceased to exist as an independent town.

The next four pages show:

A view of Lower Pulteneytown taken from Sillarsburn on the north side of the river. Boats can be seen lying above the swing bridge, known as the Service Bridge. This was the first planned industrial town in Scotland and until the 1870s all the curing in Wick was done either here or around the harbour and bay. When this photograph was taken there were 15 companies curing in the eight main streets. The largest was the company of Andrew Bremner which occupied about 1/15th of the area between the harbour and the saw mill, upriver, by itself. He was the most successful curer in Wick's history and owned similar establishments in all the major herring ports.

The transfer of the administration made little or no difference to the way in which the town's industry functioned and the future seemed as assured as ever. Perhaps more than ever because only three years before this union one of the significant events of the decade had taken place. On the 5th of July, 1899 there had steamed into Wick the first locally owned steam drifter, the 'Content' skippered by Alex Thain. She was shortly followed by the 'Peep o'Day' and by 1905 of a total fleet of 313, 25 were steam drifters. And all over the coast of the country there was a dramatic switch from sail to steam, and after a few years motor. By 1910 there were only 169 sailing boats left and in 1923 there were only 10.

The advent of steam and motor had a great influence over the decline of the fleet but it was by no means the only one.

At its peak in the 1840's and 50's the population of the county had stood at 44,000 as all the villages, and the districts around them had blossomed in the wake of the success of the herring fishing. But they were the first to feel the effects of the innovations such as the increase in the size of the craft and the other changes. Most of the country people lived on crofts, mostly very small and, without the extra money provided by the sea, hopelessly uneconomic. As the industry began to concentrate with a quickening pace on Wick, Lybster, Dunbeath and Helmsdale the crofter fishermen found more and more difficulty in dispensing of their catches. Schooners no longer called at their local stations and this, along with the difficulties arising as their local cooperages closed, left them with the choice of either giving up the fishing or moving to one of the larger ports. Many did seek employment there but this involved being away from home for long periods or walking, as many did, up to 20 miles at the weekend to get home. But a few greater attractions was being offered.

Countries such as Canada, Australia and South Africa were opening up and adverts appeared in the local paper offering enormous amounts of land for little or nothing with the prospect of wonder-

The fleet leaving about 1910. BF.1459 Success of Portessie and BF.466 Helena of Portknockie in the foreground. The men on the large Zulu are holding the wands which were used to pole her out until the wind caught the sails.

Gutters in Calder's yard Shaltigoe in the 1860s. There were 5000 lassies gutting herring in Wick.

Barrels were repacked and topped up after a few days. Water's yard at the Camps.

ful opportunity. Farming on a prairie, on hundreds of acres seemed vastly more attractive to a crofter who was struggling to raise a family of up to 10 on 16 acres of hard, rocky ground. And they left in their hundreds for the cities and overseas. Not only from the country but from the villages and towns to the extent that by 1910 the population had fallen by 17,000. One of the first things the emigrants did in their new country was to form a Caithness Association to remind themselves of the county that they had left so eagerly.

The steam drifter, although Wick fishermen never adopted them on the scale of the fishermen on the south side of the Moray Firth, held out a great deal more promise than it actually delivered. It was a well designed boat and had every convenience that the sailing vessels could not offer. It was impervious to the absence of wind and was ideal for winter fishings which had been growing in importance for the last 30 years. In 1901 a sailing boat cost between £7-800 while a drifter of comparable size was £2000-£3000. It could burn up to 20 tons of coal a week, and in the 1920's Wick coal merchants would deliver up to 8000 tons of coal in a week, all in 1 cwt. bags, a total of 160,000 bags.

Sailing boats of course incurred no expenses while at sea but as it happened the period between 1900 and 1912, when most of the construction of steam drifters was undertaken, was one of the most sustained periods of prosperity that the fishing had ever known. As such the costs of running these large expensive boats were not as noticeable as they were to become in the slump that followed the First World War.

An early type of dual purpose motor boat, the Venus the first to be built by D. Alexander and Co.

The first Wick boat to be converted from sail to an oil engine was the 'Crystal River' which had an engine installed in 1906. Many others were soon to follow although by comparison with the steam engines they were very small and much less powerful. But since they were mainly required to provide the boat with the seaway to get to the fishing grounds and back, the comparative slowness did not matter as many still carried their sails to complement the engines. Neither the steam drifters nor the converted sailing boats could match the speed of one of the large Fifies or Zulus under full sail in the right weather conditions. A drifter could do about 8 knots and were frequently passed by the vessels who still kept their sails. An outstanding example of sailing ability of both the boats and their crews was given in 1903 when Jim Baikie sailed the ' Alexandra,' a large Fifie, from Wick to Yarmouth, a distance of nearly 460 miles, in 42½ hours, quay to quay. This time has never been broken by a fishing vessel. But like their contemporaries, the extreme clipper, events overtook them and the large sailing herring drifters never enjoyed the success for the length of time that their design and construction deserved.

The fishings up to the beginning of the First World War were extemely successful in Wick. The exporters, and there were still about 90 different companies in the town who were aggressively selling their products all over Europe and beyond, could harly keep up with the demand. Wick cured herring was going by the tens and thousands of barrels, which were being manufactured by 400 coopers, and kippers were leaving by the train load for the Pacific and Orient liners, the Cunard line and the British India company. Curers were entering, and winning prizes for their products, in exhibitions in Paris, Vienna, Stettin and Salzburg. And a new company Marvis, which had set up in the old wool

The fleet in the early 1920s. A herring net is spread on the wharf which was built over the slipway visible in earlier photographs.

Filling up the barrels in Davidson and Pirie's yard at the bottom of Rutherford Street, in the 1920s.

Landing at the north quay.

mills, was exporting canned herring and their own speciality, dried flake codfish, which could be re-constituted by adding water. Another company was experimenting with something they called Rossl-ings, after the proprietor, which was a kind of fish finger. Yet another was making fish sausages. The main boatbuilding yard had changed to the construction of steel drifters, although only half a dozen were built altogether, both steel and wooden.

Things carried on like this till a blow, in the shape of the First World War, landed on the herring industry. One which, incredible as it may have seemed to those in the trade at the time, signalled that it was moving into the last 40 years of its existence.

Most of the fishermen joined the services, mainly the navy, although towards the end of the war many were drafted into the army to replace the losses incurred on the French Battlefields. A few boats, crewed by men who were too old for active service contrived to catch herring during the war and they did very well, generally, as the food shortages caused by the German blockade of the Atlan-tic sent the price of herring up to levels that had previously been undreamed of. But not all the boats were lucky enough to share among the high prices. There was a large minefield just off Clythness, forming part of the outer defences of Scapa Flow, the large naval base in Orkney, and the drifter 'Maggie Parker' struck a mine when it became entangled in her nets. She and her crew vanished without trace.

Many of the Wick boats had been commissioned by the admiralty to serve as ferries and tenders to the battleships in Scapa Flow and many of the older fishermen were stationed there. One Wick drifter 'The Mayberry' was the tender which took Lord Kitchener from Scrabster to join the cruiser

The Nimrod, an early seine netter lying at the river jetties.

'Hampshire' for his ill-fated voyage to Russia, which was to end in tragedy only a few miles away on the coast of Hoy. This same drifter was also involved in a furious enquiry which took place in Scapa Flow itself, when one of the crew appropriated a particularly fine cod that had been destined, and had appeared on the menu, for Admiral Beattie. The mystery has never been officially solved by the navy. The return of the peace in 1918 saw what looked like the resumption of business as usual once the fishermen, or those who had survived the war, returned. But a series of heavy blows again landed on the industry in the next twenty years.

The first, which was again to prove a portentious year for the industry came in 1922 with the collapse of the Deutchmark. A great deal of herring had been exported during that and the previous year to Germany, a country which was literally starving under the weight of War Reparations being extracted by the French, mainly. The desperate Germans were offering higher prices than their rivals to ensure supplies and their economy was rapidly deteriorating, causing a continuous devaluation of the currency. Latterly it was worthless and bales and bales of money arrived in Wick, and many other towns, to pay for the purchases. Fish curers, and of course fishermen with them, went bankrupt by the dozen. One, Mr Gordon Dower, who till that time had been a prosperous curer retained enough of his sense of humour to use the notes he had received to paper a room in his house with them on the grounds that he had always wanted to be able to do such a thing.

And that same year in Wick a new form of fishing, which had never been undertaken before, made its first appearance. It was eventually to supercede the herring fishing. It was begun by Mr William Waters in his drifter 'Fairy Hill' and he was soon followed by one of the outstanding seamen

The arrival of the drifters in the late 1930's. The harbour master is on the point of the north quay directing them to their berths and his assistant, Neil Stewart, is on the south quay.

A boat landing coal with buckets which the stevedores filled by shovel in the hold.

The launch of the Two Boys one of the last boats built by D Alexander. She was pushed manually on rollers from his yard 100 yards to the launch site down river, and pulled over the edge of the quay by Messrs Allan's steam traction engine, visible on the north bank of the river.

Three Danish fishing vessels moored outside a converted Zulu in the inner harbour. E.280 was the Ellen which took the bodies of the crew of the Metha back to Denmark. The Metha was lost at the harbour mouth in 1934.

From the hold to the quay.

of the day, Mr William Thain in his drifter ' Zoe.' He was the son of the man who had sailed the first steam drifter into Wick, 23 years before. Steam drifters were not at all suited for seine net fishing and it would not be long before the yards were turning over to the construction of dual purpose boats, which could pursue either the herring or seine net fishing.

Even as the struggle to shake off the losses from Germany was going on, yet another calamity overcame the industry, to be followed by yet another.

The first was the civil and social upheaval in Russia when the Bolshevics finally won through and took control of the country. Russia was an important market but for a few years after Stalin succeeded Lenin the herring which Russia imported was not always paid for as the agent who had contracted the cargo had nearly always been liquidated and no one else would assume responsibility for payment. Even the curers who had the financial resources to withstand the losses of the German faulure were finding it difficult to keep going especially when their other troubles were closely followed by the international slump, the worst of all. Not only did the bottom fall out of the market but this time coincided with poor fishings, and fishermen went bankrupt in hundreds around the coasts.

A paralysing depression, in every form, gripped the industry. Drifters could be bought, coaled up, ready for the sea for £40 and hundreds were sold for scrap when the fishermen could not affort to carry out even simple repairs. In Wick it was no different, except that, proportionately speaking, there were not so many steam drifters to dispose of. There were still quite a few of the old converted sailing boats but there were also beginning to appear a much smaller class of boat, between 40 and 50 feet, which was turning more and more to seine net.

Herring on its way to the yards. Coal merchants hired out their carts during the season.

The launch of the Fisher Boy from the yard of D. Alexander in Wick River. The pilot boat acted as the tug.

A crate of Marvis on its way to the navy.

The shed in the middle of the barrels was a first aid post and rest station for the lassies.

The open mouthed barrels were called kits and used to transport the herring to the yards.

The seine net had many economic advantages over the herring fishing. Firstly, only half the crew, or even less were needed, four or five men as opposed to 10 or 12 on a drifter. A very important matter to fishermen whose wages depended on the division of the profits. Where a drifter needed 100 nets, a seine net boat shot only one, with another three or four as spares. It could also shoot its nets once an hour, and move to other grounds if there was no fish. Drifters could only shoot their nets once, it could take six or more hours to haul them, and there might be no fish in them after that. All in all the economic factors were in the seine net boat's favour with the exception that if a drifter struck large shoals of herring it could make enormous amounts of money, if the catch could be sold, which in the 1930s was not at all certain.

During the mid 1930s, almost as many herring were dumped unsold in Wick Bay as were sold for curing. It is not a very encouraging prospect to reflect that a boat could be 10 hours hauling a shot of herring and then spend five hours dumping them when they arrived in the harbour. Yet that is what happened, frequently, and more frequently than the industry in general and the fishermen in particular could withstand.

The Wick fleet continued to shrink and some were sold to scrap merchants for use as ferries to take the non-ferrous scrap from the salvaged German fleet in Scapa Flow, to the dealers in the south. Several of them sank, taking men with them, when the new owners recklessly overloaded them as they tried to meet the demand for scrap caused by the re-armament programme.

There was a brief flurry of activity in the last three years before the outbreak of war, but this was due almost entirely to visiting vessels as the Wick herring fleet could no longer sustain the shore based operations by itself. Of course visiting vessels had always played a part in the Wick fishing, but for the first time, the curers had to depend on the arrival of stranger vessels to keep their businesses going. After the war was finished this was to prove the undoing, with other factors, of the industry in Wick. By 1939 the Wick fleet had lost nearly 270 boats since 1900.

There was no herring fishing at all during the Second World War and only a few seine net and small handline boats fished during this period. As in the First World War they were manned by crews who were too old to serve in the armed forces. Yet two of the Wick steam drifters, the 'Lottie' and the 'Isabella Ferguson' were retained in the harbour during the war for use as blockships in the event of invasion. They were never used for this purpose and were broken up in Broadhaven just as the war finished. They and the 'Sweet Pea' had been the last steam drifters to fish under the Wick registration. The last sailboat was the 'City of Paris,' skippered by William Miller, father-in-law of William Thain, and she had foundered in Sinclair Bay in 1924.

When the young men returned from the war there was a false dawn when it looked as if the herring fishing might, given time, prosper again. For three years, 1947 to 1950 there was a visiting fleet, from both Scotland and England of about 50 steam drifters augmenting the local fleet of about 10 dual purpose boats which gave up seine net fishing during the summer to follow the herring. The rest of the fleet of about 35 boats continued with seine netting. There were still about 60 coopers working in the town and 300 or so fisher lassies. This was to be the last time, after nearly 180 years, that Gaelic speaking fisher lassies were to come to Wick.

But the times were changing fast. There was no longer the demand for salted herrings as the social upheavals of the war had brought a revolution in diets, working contitions, opportunities and everything else. Work at the herring, whether afloat or ashore, was dirty and heavy, and offered irregular hours, sometimes with no pay if no fish were landed. The old methods could not stand against the sweeping changes that were taking place and were turned aside by forces which were beyond their control. The last year in which the fishing in Wick was conducted in its traditional form could be said to be 1953. Thereafter the remaining curers switched to the processing of whitefish and the greatly reduced workforce that this required. A few small boats in Lybster and Dunbeath went to the inshore fishing for a couple of years afterwards, but this too slowly died out.

The last Wick owned herring drifter, a motor boat built as a dual purpose vessel was the 'Fisher Boy,' skippered and owned by Jimmy Bremner who ceased fishing for herring in 1953.

So the old yards fell silent for the last time. In common with its smaller neighbours, who earlier had felt the cold hand of failure, Wick's herring trade passed over the horizon between reality and memory.